CW01512505

Original title:

Hazy Filters Over the Dragon Jut

Copyright © 2025 Swan Charm

All rights reserved.

Author: Paulina Pähkel

ISBN HARDBACK: 978-1-80562-548-3

ISBN PAPERBACK: 978-1-80564-069-1

Through Soft Glimmers

In twilight's glow, the shadows play,
Whispers of secrets, night holds sway.
Stars in the distance begin to wane,
Dreams take flight, breaking the chain.

Among the leaves, a soft wind sighs,
Time drifts slowly, as magic flies.
Crickets serenade the harbor of night,
With wishes and hopes, their voices ignite.

Myths Awaken

Under the moon, legends arise,
With flickering flames that light the skies.
Tales of old dance in the air,
Echoes of magic, beyond compare.

From whispers of giants, to elves so fair,
Each story woven with delicate care.
Truth and fable entwined like lace,
In the heart of the woods, a forgotten place.

Reflections on the Edge of Fog

Misty tendrils cradle the dawn,
In silence, the world holds a yawn.
Reflections shimmer on puddles deep,
Secrets kept by shadows that creep.

Each step forward, a tale unfolds,
Wisdom of ages in whispers told.
Through veils of grey, the past arrives,
Where hope lingers and magic thrives.

Beneath a Gossamer Veil of Wonder

Beneath the stars, a tapestry spun,
Threads of enchantment, one by one.
Gossamer whispers weave through the trees,
Carrying dreams on a gentle breeze.

The world awakens, bathed in light,
As shadows retreat from the dawn's first bite.
In the heart of a realm so grand,
Magic resides in the palm of your hand.

Dance of the Elusive Serpent's Breath

In twilight's ballroom, shadows embrace,
A serpent glides in a silken trace.
With every pulse, the air ignites,
Whispers of dreams in the softest nights.

Around and around, the dance unfolds,
Lost in the rhythm, where time beholds.
Elusive and rare, like a fleeting sigh,
In the heart of the night, let spirits fly.

The Forgotten Choir Beneath the Smoke

In shadows deep where whispers weave,
A choir sings, yet none believe.
Beneath the smoke, their echoes float,
Lost melodies in silence wrote.

Once they soared on wings of light,
Now bound by dusk, they lose their sight.
Each note a shard of stories past,
A haunting hymn that fades too fast.

The stars above, a distant glow,
They yearn for warmth, but chill winds blow.
In forgotten corners, they lament,
The dreams of ages, long since spent.

Yet in the dark, a spark ignites,
Awakening the dormant nights.
With breath held tight, they raise their plea,
For someone brave to set them free.

So wander forth, oh curious soul,
Through veils of mist to find the whole.
For when you listen, hearts engage,
The choir sings from every page.

Secrets Held by Time's Guardian

In ancient halls where shadows dwell,
A guardian keeps the stories well.
With eyes like stars, they watch the flow,
Of time's own dance, both fast and slow.

With every tick, a memory tides,
In whispered winds, the secret hides.
They cradle dreams of those long gone,
And weave their tales with dawn's first song.

The echoes ring on golden strands,
Of battles fought in distant lands.
Through whispered lore and timeless grace,
The guardian holds a sacred space.

So step with care on paths unseen,
For every shadow may yet glean.
A chance to glimpse what once has been,
In city's heart or forest green.

With tender heart and fearless mind,
A secret's key is what you'll find.
Embrace the tales, let them unwind,
For time's own guardian whispers kind.

Veils of Mist Above the Peaks

Veils of mist dance, soft and bright,
In the early glow of morning light.
Whispers of dreams take flight with grace,
As nature's charm begins to trace.

Mountains loom, their spirits awake,
Bathed in hues that silence makes.
Each shadowed crag holds tales untold,
In the embrace of the mist, so bold.

The world below, a fleeting thought,
Here, the heart finds what it sought.
A tranquil beauty captures the soul,
In the mountains, one becomes whole.

Shadows Embrace the Fiery Ridge

Shadows cling to the fiery ridge,
Where sunlight dances, a fleeting bridge.
Crimson hues bleed into the night,
As day sighs softly, fading from sight.

Echoes of laughter, the wind does bear,
Stories of old, spun with care.
The earth below, a steadfast friend,
Guiding the heart where dreams ascend.

Fires burn with a searing glow,
Casting silhouettes that ebb and flow.
In this twilight dance, all is revealed,
The secrets of life gently healed.

Whispers of Smoke in the Twilight

Whispers of smoke drift through the trees,
Carried softly by the evening breeze.
They curl and twist in a spectral waltz,
Each puff of mystery, a world that faults.

Beneath the stars, shadows take flight,
In the twilight's embrace, merging with night.
Each ember glows like a lingering thought,
In the silence, connection is sought.

A flickering flame, a heart's desire,
Kindled beneath the vast expanse of wire.
As dreams unravel in smoky trails,
The night whispers softly, as magic prevails.

The Veiled Summit's Secrets

The veiled summit holds secrets deep,
Where ancient echoes of the past creep.
Every stone whispers tales of lore,
Of those who climbed and sought for more.

Wrapped in clouds, the peak looms high,
Where wishes are cast like stars in the sky.
In the chill of the air, a promise lingers,
As destiny beckons with unseen fingers.

Glimmers of truth reside in the mist,
Much like a lover's forgotten kiss.
Through trials faced and journeys unfurled,
The summit holds the heart of the world.

The Drift of Dreams in Mystic Air

In the hush of night, whispers weave,
Stars twinkle softly, secrets they leave.
Clouds drift like thoughts in a gentle stream,
Carrying wishes, the thread of a dream.

Moonlight spills silver on a quiet glade,
Where shadows lean close, their dance never swayed.
The breeze hums a melody, sweet and rare,
Telling tales of enchantment that linger in air.

Softening Touch of the Forgotten Sky

The sun dips low with a warm, golden grin,
Wrapping the world in a soft, tender skin.
Clouds blush with colors that fade into night,
As stars shyly bloom, a magical sight.

In the silence, echoes of laughter take flight,
While day yields to dreams, softening light.
The sky holds memories of what once was true,
In its gentle embrace, we are born anew.

Beyond the Glimmering Gates of Legend

Where tales of valor and dragons reside,
Beyond silver gates where the brave ones abide.
Echoes of bravery in the cool, crisp air,
Whispers of legends, beyond compare.

Through paths of stardust and shimmering light,
The brave hearts assemble, ready for flight.
With courage as armor and dreams as their sword,
They venture forth, ever true to their word.

Shadows Dance in the Twilight's Embrace

When twilight descends, and the world grows dim,
The shadows awaken with a delicate whim.
They twirl through the thickets, a mystical waltz,
Unraveling secrets and timeless faults.

With a sigh of the stars, the night sings a tune,
As shadows lay quiet under the moon.
They whisper of stories, both tender and bold,
In the embrace of the twilight, mysteries unfold.

The Silent Reverie of Firelit Memory

In the glow of embers bright,
Whispers dance, embracing night.
A flicker trails through shadowed halls,
Echoes soft as evening calls.

Laughter fades like mist on glass,
Moments held, yet none can pass.
Time weaves tales of joy and fear,
In flames that turn to silent tears.

Beneath the stars, the heart shall yearn,
For every lesson, every turn.
Memories flicker, soft and low,
In this warm and ancient glow.

With every spark, the past ignites,
Stories woven through endless nights.
Carried forth on an ageless breeze,
Silent reverie brings us ease.

So gather round, let fire speak,
Of love once strong, now bittersweet.
In shadows deep, find peace we crave,
In silent reveries, hearts behave.

Celestial Mists on the Great Wings

Upon a dawn, a silence stirs,
With whispers soft as feathered furs.
Celestial mists in colors bright,
Hover gently, painting light.

Great wings flap in the azure sky,
Bearing dreams, as they drift by.
A symphony of hope and grace,
Held aloft in an endless space.

The heart soars high, in flight it gleams,
Chasing after woven dreams.
Through clouds and winds, it seeks to find,
The secrets of the beautiful mind.

Each moment laced with magic's thread,
Casts vibrant colors where it treads.
In every heartbeat, joy persists,
Among the mists, the soul exists.

So let us rise on wings of light,
In dreams and wonders, find our height.
With mists so soft, we'll surely glide,
On celestial wings, forever ride.

Hidden Realms of the Fiery Serpent

Beneath the earth, where shadows loom,
A fiery serpent stirs from gloom.
With scales aglow like molten gold,
It guards the secrets, ancient, bold.

In hidden realms, the echoes play,
Of whispered tales from yesterday.
Through caverns deep, its spirit coils,
While mystery in silence toils.

A flicker of flame, a glimmer bright,
Guides the brave through darkest night.
In riddles spun by time's embrace,
The serpent finds its rightful place.

In each heartbeat, the fire sighs,
As torches flicker, raising cries.
Legends born from embered light,
In hidden realms, they dance in flight.

So dare to delve where few have tread,
In search of truths that lie ahead.
For in the dark, the serpent waits,
With fiery whispers to unlock fates.

In the Grasp of Darkened Skies

When twilight falls, and shadows creep,
The world is lost in dreams so deep.
Stars twinkle softly, lost in grace,
While night unfolds its velvet lace.

In the grasp of darkened skies,
Whispers linger, somber sighs.
A tapestry of night unfurled,
Embracing thoughts from a weary world.

Through moonlit paths, the lost shall roam,
Finding solace far from home.
In stillness, echoes rise and blend,
As night becomes a timeless friend.

In every shadow, stories hide,
Of laughter once and tears long dried.
A whispered tale across the night,
In darkness born, yet yearning light.

So close your eyes to night's sweet call,
In darkened skies, we rise, we fall.
With dreams that linger, soft and shy,
To dance forever where shadows lie.

Shrouded Glories of the Distant Ridgeline

Across the ridgeline, shadows creep,
Whispers of secrets that the mountains keep.
In the misty shroud, a tale unfolds,
Of glories hidden, of bravery bold.

Once fierce and bright, the stars align,
Lost in the echoes of a distant time.
Their laughter dances on the wind's breath,
Reminders of life beyond the veil of death.

Rocky cliffs guard the ancient lore,
Stories etched in stone forevermore.
With every step upon this ground,
A symphony of silence sings profound.

Beneath the sky, where dusk descends,
The ridgeline holds what darkness lends.
In every shadow, a glimmer awaits,
A spark of magic that time creates.

So heed the call when twilight beams,
For shrouded glories live in dreams.
With heart alight and spirit free,
Awake the tales that yearn to be.

Dull Pulse of Ancient Legends

In the heart of the woods, silence reigns,
Echoes of legends in hidden lanes.
The forest breathes a weary sigh,
As whispers swirl, and memories fly.

Beneath the roots, a story lies,
Of lovers lost and faithful ties.
Each branch a witness to love and strife,
Pulsing softly with the heartbeat of life.

Time-worn tomes in the library dim,
Conceal the truth within each hymn.
Like shadows lingering at dusk's embrace,
These ancient tales leave a haunting trace.

Flickering lights in the distance glow,
Guiding spirits that wander slow.
Through tangled paths where the wild things creep,
Awaken the legends from their sleep.

So listen closely when night unveils,
The dulcet tones of forgotten trails.
For in the murmur of nature's breath,
Lie echoes of life, and whispers of death.

Veils of Night on Forgotten Wings

The night unfurls its velvet cloak,
On wings of whispers, soft and broke.
In shadows deep where dreams take flight,
Veils of night evoke a mystic sight.

Eyes of stars peek through the haze,
Guiding seekers in a delicate maze.
Their twinkling tales of long-lost lore,
With every beat, yearn to explore.

Through silvered branches, moonlight drips,
Casting spells on the dreaming lips.
Each sigh that rides the twilight breeze,
Carries secrets from ancient trees.

Forgotten beings with stories wide,
On the wings of night, they softly glide.
In the hush of dark, old histories breathe,
Bound by the magic that they weave.

So dare to wander where shadows play,
In the folds of night that drift away.
For in those veils, the past awakes,
And in its depths, a new path makes.

Embers Submerged in Gloomy Dreams

In the depths of night, embers glow,
Hints of warmth in a world of woe.
Beneath the blanket of sorrow's song,
Lie whispers of courage, steady and strong.

Buried thoughts in twilight's haze,
Dance like phantoms in a foggy maze.
Each flicker tells of battles fought,
In the quiet heart where hope is sought.

Amidst the shadows, a flicker stirs,
A flicker that thrives when all else blurs.
With tender light, it guides the way,
Through the depths of despair, towards the day.

So gather your dreams, let them ignite,
In the gloomiest corners, find your light.
For embers submerged can rise anew,
Breaking chains and breathing true.

In every heart, a fire resides,
Waiting for winds to turn the tides.
Embrace the warmth, let spirits gleam,
For in the dark, we nurture dreams.

The Whispering Mists of Eldritch Heights

In the vale where shadows play,
Whispers ride the winds of gray.
Mysteries dance in twilight's gleam,
Eldritch secrets softly dream.

Ancient stones with stories old,
Guard the tales of brave and bold.
Echoes linger, breaths of lore,
Calling forth the hearts that soar.

Moonlight bathes the winding path,
Casting spells that feed the wrath.
Eldritch heights, where spirits roam,
Boundless magic finds its home.

Fables woven in the mist,
Long-forgotten tales persist.
Beneath the stars, adventures thrill,
Echoing hearts with steadfast will.

Twilight Dreams and Scaled Secrets

In twilight's fold, the secrets hide,
Dreams awaken, darkness chides.
Scales that shimmer in the night,
Guard the treasures, pure and bright.

Whispers soft as dragon's breath,
Tell of life entwined with death.
Mystic echoes guide the way,
Through the shadows where sprites play.

Underneath the silver skies,
Scaled beasts soar with ancient cries.
In their flight, the tales unfold,
Of hidden worlds and hearts of gold.

Twilight dreams of realms unseen,
Woven threads of fate between.
In the hush before the dawn,
Secrets linger, softly drawn.

Secrets Hidden in the Luminous Fog

In luminous fog, the lost reside,
Secrets gleam where shadows bide.
Whispers of the night, they speak,
Revealing truths that wander, seek.

Faint glimmers illuminate the track,
Guiding souls who dare not look back.
Past the veil of misty grey,
Hidden wonders wait to play.

Footfalls echo on the ground,
In the stillness, magic's found.
Every breath a spell, a lore,
Opening enchanted door.

In the fog, the dreamers roam,
Seeking paths to call their home.
With every step, the secrets grow,
In that luminous mist, aglow.

Fables Cloaked in Ethereal Light

In ethereal light, the fables twine,
Crafted whispers, pure and divine.
Stories echo, soft and clear,
Chanting truths for those who hear.

Cloaked in mist, the legends rise,
Stars above in watchful skies.
Each tale spun with threads of gold,
Offers warmth against the cold.

Through the night, the verses soar,
Binding hearts forevermore.
In the glow of dawn's embrace,
Fables find their rightful place.

A tapestry of dreams, so bright,
In the silence, pure delight.
Magic dances, takes its flight,
In the fables cloaked in light.

Mysteries of the Shrouded Summit

In shadows deep where whispers dwell,
The ancient stones hold secrets well.
Beneath the moon's soft, silver gaze,
The echoes weave enchanted ways.

The paths are lost, entwined in mist,
With every turn, a tale subsists.
A breeze may carry voices low,
Of legends masked in twilight's glow.

Above the peaks, the spirits fly,
In silent grace, they dance and sigh.
'Tis here the stars conspire and meet,
In twilight's arms, life's threads repeat.

The summit waits, both wise and old,
With mysteries that remain untold.
Adventurers heed the call of night,
For magic stirs in the fading light.

A shrouded world, so vast, so grand,
Awaits those bold enough to stand.
Upon the brink, where dreams reside,
A journey beckons, far and wide.

Enigmatic Breezes Through Dragon Valleys

In valleys deep where shadows glide,
The whispers dance as legends bide.
A breath of fate through ancient stone,
Where fire and secrets find their own.

The dragons soar with graceful might,
Their scales aglow in fading light.
Each flap of wing, a tale unfolds,
Of warriors brave and treasures bold.

The winds are laced with echoes bright,
A haunting song throughout the night.
Their melodies in twilight's clasp,
Invite the wanderers to grasp.

Through gorges wide, the dreams take flight,
In realms where all is dark and light.
The valleys cradle secrets deep,
Within their hold, the heroes sleep.

With every breath, a story calls,
Through dragon's dreams and ancient halls.
Where shadows play and light brings cheer,
The enigmatic waits, ever near.

Silhouettes of Majesty in Soft Fog

In softest fog where giants loom,
Their silhouettes dispel the gloom.
The landscape breathes a silent sigh,
While echoes of the ancients fly.

Majestic forms in mist entwined,
With secrets dark within their mind.
An aura rich of whispered lore,
Of battles fought on distant shore.

The rolling hills, a canvas wide,
With nature's brush, the colors hide.
Yet in the dusk, they softly glow,
As twilight weaves a tale below.

In every bend, a story waits,
In shadows cast by unseen fates.
A tapestry of dreams unfurls,
As time stands still in breathless whirls.

Enshrined in fog, the world spins slow,
In silhouettes where secrets flow.
The majesty of nature's hand,
Awaits the brave to understand.

The Enfolding Whisper of Colorful Clouds

Above the world, in skies so bright,
The clouds weave tales of pure delight.
In hues that shift from gray to gold,
They embrace the dreams yet untold.

A whisper floats on gentle breeze,
As colors swirl 'neath ancient trees.
The heavens dance, a playful sight,
Inviting souls to join the flight.

With every shade, a story spins,
Of hope reborn and where it begins.
Through azure arcs and rosy dawn,
The spirit of adventure's drawn.

In twilight's grace, they gather round,
The secrets of the skies abound.
The clouds enfold the fleeting day,
In whispered tones, they fade away.

And as the night begins to creep,
In cozy folds, the heavens sleep.
The colors merge, a dreamer's mend,
Where whispers linger, never end.

Flickering Hues Beyond the Mist

In the dawn's embrace, colors dance,
Whispers of magic in each glance.
The fog retreats, unveiling light,
Painting the world with hues so bright.

Leaves shimmer softly, gold and green,
Nature's canvas in every scene.
A breeze carries secrets from the glade,
In this realm where dreams are made.

Birds take flight, their song a thrill,
Echoing gently on the hill.
With every pulse of morning's grace,
Life awakens in this sacred space.

Crimson trails mark the path we tread,
In twilight's hush, where shadows spread.
Glimmers of hope in every sigh,
Cascades of wonder fill the sky.

As daylight wanes, the stars ignite,
Guiding us gently into the night.
Flickering hues in the mist's embrace,
Forever etched in time and space.

The Sorrowful Roar of the Enshrouded Behemoth

Through the valleys, a mournful sound,
Echoes of fury that shake the ground.
The behemoth stirs in the hidden deep,
Guarding the secrets it longs to keep.

Cloaked in shadows, it moves with grace,
Memories hidden behind its face.
With every roar, a tale is spun,
Of battles lost and victories won.

Blackened storms brew above its head,
Whispers of fears left long unsaid.
In the stillness, the world holds its breath,
Awaiting the release of its wretched depth.

Ancient trees tremble, their roots take hold,
As the creature's sorrow begins to unfold.
In the heart of the forest, despair entwines,
The essence of time in haunting lines.

Yet, in the darkest of nights, hope remains,
A flicker of light in the endless pains.
For within the roar dwells a yearning heart,
To bridge the divide, to heal the part.

Cinders Fleeting in the Gentle Darkness

Silent embers in twilight glow,
Whispers of warmth in soft shadows flow.
Cinders drifting on the night breeze,
Carrying stories on the rustling trees.

Memories linger in the hazy air,
Echoes of laughter, shadows of care.
In the depths of night, secrets unfold,
Hearts intertwine as the darkness grows bold.

Each flickering flame a silent plea,
To capture the moments that long to be free.
In this gentle darkness, dreams ignite,
Lighting the path through the silent night.

Dance of the fireflies, fleeting light,
Guided by starlust, soft and bright.
In the embrace of the midnight shade,
Life spins softly in the theater made.

And when the dawn spills gold anew,
The cinders fade, as all things do.
Yet in the heart, those embers remain,
Glowing forever in a transient chain.

The Murmur of Love in the Ashen Air

Amidst the ruins, a tender sigh,
Where ancient flames have bid goodbye.
In the ashen air, love finds a tune,
Soft as the whispers of the waning moon.

Echoes of warmth in the chilling night,
Hearts intertwined in fading light.
With every murmur, hope takes flight,
Casting shadows that shimmer bright.

Fingers entwined, we walk the lane,
Through memories etched in joy and pain.
In the quiet, our hearts embark,
Illuminating the world's dark arc.

The ashes cradle our timeless dreams,
In the silence, love's soft gleams.
For in the rubble, we've sown our seeds,
Nurturing life through our shared needs.

As dawn approaches, new light appears,
Washing away our doubts and fears.
In the ashen air, our vows remain,
The sweet murmur of love's gentle reign.

Phantoms of Flame in Dreamy Shrouds

In the stillness, whispers creep,
Dancing shadows, secrets keep.
Fires flicker in twilight's grace,
Veils of dreams, a hidden place.

Ghostly figures waltz in night,
Breath of embers, hearts alight.
Through the mist, they glide and sway,
Lost in echoes, come what may.

With every gust, the flames will bloom,
Casting charms that pierce the gloom.
Phantoms laugh, as chill winds sigh,
In the dark, they twirl and fly.

Rustling leaves sing soft refrains,
Chasing whispers 'round the lanes.
The air is thick with dreams aflame,
All who wander, seek their name.

As dawn breaks, the phantoms fade,
Into the light, their dances laid.
Yet in the heart, their fire stays,
A smoldering spark in sunlit rays.

The Clouded Crown of the Skyward Beast

Above the earth, where shadows lie,
A beast with wings will soar and sigh.
Cloaked in clouds, with eyes of night,
A crown of storms, a fearsome sight.

Majestic roars crack through the air,
Its thunderous heart, a tempest rare.
Darkened skies twist in its wake,
The world beneath begins to shake.

Gales entwine in furious dance,
Caught in the grip of fate's wild chance.
Wonders hidden in swirling mist,
A creature born of legend's tryst.

Yet in the storm's chaotic reach,
Ancient secrets rise to breach.
Whispers of magic, lost to time,
Bind the clouds in rhythm and rhyme.

So watch the skies, ye brave and bold,
For tales of yore in midnight's hold.
The clouded crown shall always reign,
A guardian force, both wise and arcane.

Illusions Dancing on Smoky Valleys

In valleys deep where shadows play,
Illusions weave the light of day.
Mist wraps around each fleeting form,
A twinkle here, a whisper warm.

Figures shift, like flickering flames,
Concealing truths in whispered games.
Every step, a chance to fall,
In smoky dreams that softly call.

Winds carry laughter, soft as air,
Revealing glimpses — a ghostly fare.
The past entwined with moments new,
Every breath, a phantom's view.

Beyond the haze, a glimmer bright,
Awaits the heart's long-lost delight.
Yet shadows linger, ever near,
In smoky valleys, tinged with fear.

But take a step, and you may find,
The world is shaped by hearts entwined.
Illusions dance, yet truth remains,
In the echo of familiar names.

Enchanted Gloom Over Ancient Heights

On ancient heights where shadows sigh,
Enchanted gloom ascends the sky.
Logs of legends, thick with lore,
Call to spirits, forevermore.

Brambles twist in twilight's hold,
Guardians stand, both fierce and bold.
Whispers float upon the breeze,
From long-lost souls beneath the trees.

Stars above weave tales of night,
Casting dreams in soft starlight.
In the gloom, a magic hums,
A symphony of time that comes.

Mountains cradle every sound,
Echoes of ages wrap around.
In the silence, find your place,
Amidst the shadows, feel the grace.

As dawn unfolds, the shadows fade,
Yet in your heart, the dreams cascade.
For every height holds stories deep,
In enchanted gloom, our wishes keep.

The Lament of Ember's Halo

In the deep of night, a whisper calls,
Where ember's glow and darkness falls.
A tale of woe on the winds is spun,
Of battles lost and dreams undone.

The stars above, in silence weep,
For secrets buried, shadows keep.
A halo bright once warmed the hearts,
Now flickers dim, as hope departs.

A phantom echo, lost in time,
Casts shadows where the light once shined.
The fireflies dance, but dance alone,
For in this night, their light has flown.

As listed leaves on autumn ground,
Memories whisper, yet no sound.
Ember's light still seeks the dawn,
While in the dark, the dreams are drawn.

So take this song, a weary plea,
For all who long to be set free.
In shadows deep, let courage stay,
For every night must yield to day.

Shadowed Glories of the Forgotten Realm

In the hush of twilight, echoes sing,
Of a realm where forgotten glories cling.
Whispers weave through ancient trees,
Bound by magic carried on the breeze.

In the heart of shadows, secrets hide,
Where the lost and lonely often bide.
Each leaf and stone, a tale to tell,
Of triumphs forged in silent hell.

The castle crumbled, its laughter ceased,
But in the silence, spirits feast.
With every stepped path, a ghost resides,
In forgotten glories, history abides.

An owl's lament on moonlit flight,
Guides the wanderer through the night.
For the weary heart that longs to roam,
In shadows deep, a light finds home.

So heed the call of the untold fate,
For in the darkness, we create.
Shadowed glories of a far-off land,
Guide us gently, hand in hand.

Breaths of Ash on Winged Dreams

In the wake of fire, ashes rise,
Like whispered wishes in autumn skies.
Each breath a story, softly spun,
Of flames that danced and races run.

With every flutter of a wing,
Hope takes flight, a gentle thing.
From smoldering past, new dreams emerge,
Carried forth on a fervent surge.

Ashen trails mark the path we take,
Guided by dreams that never break.
In flight we find a realm of grace,
New beginnings in a sacred space.

In the heart of night, a star may fall,
But wings unfurl, and dreams enthrall.
To breathe the ashes, to set them free,
Is to dance with hope, eternally.

So gather your dreams, and let them fly,
On trails of ash through the endless sky.
For in the embers' glow, we ignite,
The wings of dreams that touch the light.

Twilight's Kiss on the Scorched Heights

Up on the heights where the shadows play,
Twilight whispers of night and day.
The sun dips low, a golden guise,
Kissing the earth where the scorched land lies.

With every breath, a longing sigh,
Echoes of dreams that drift and fly.
The mountains stand where silence dwells,
Guardians of stories no tongue tells.

Cinders swirl in the gentle breeze,
Each one carries hopes like leaves on trees.
In twilight's grasp, the world awakes,
As darkness falls, the heart remakes.

The stars are born on the edges bright,
As shadows stretch and hold us tight.
Embrace the night, let go the fright,
Atop the heights, we find our light.

So heed the kiss of twilight's grace,
Let scorched heights become your space.
For every end brings forth a start,
And in the dusk, we mend the heart.

Drifting Whispers Above the Silent Ridge

In twilight's glow, the whispers weave,
Across the ridge, where shadows cleave.
Gentle breezes hum a tune,
Of hidden tales beneath the moon.

Beneath the stars, secrets sigh,
As memories in silence fly.
The mountains cradle dreams untold,
In their embrace, the night turns cold.

Each rock a sentinel, steadfast, true,
Witness to paths that wander through.
With every sigh, a story spun,
A dance of echoes, one by one.

Between the pines, the soft winds call,
Of broken hearts and whispered thrall.
A flicker here, a shadow there,
The silent ridge holds all in care.

The dawn will break, the whispers fade,
Yet in the heart, their mark is laid.
In drifting dreams and breathless night,
The silent ridge, a realm of light.

Forgotten Shadows Beneath a Fiery Sky

Beneath the blaze of twilight's fire,
Old shadows stir, igniting desire.
They dance upon the dusty ground,
In echoes lost and never found.

The evening glows with tales untold,
Of hearts once brave and souls so bold.
In every flicker, every flare,
A memory wrapped in whispers rare.

When stars emerge to take their place,
The shadows shift with ghostly grace.
They linger close, a haunting tune,
Beneath the gaze of a watchful moon.

Through fiery skies, legends fly high,
Where echoes linger, and spirits sigh.
Each story whispered, each dream seen,
In the depths of dusk, where hopes have been.

Yet dawn will break, as it must do,
And shadows fade with the morning dew.
Yet in the heart, their silent plea,
Lives on beneath the fiery spree.

The Eclipsed Heart of Scaled Giants

In caverns deep where whispers dwell,
Scaled giants slumber, under a spell.
Their hearts eclipse the light of day,
In silence wrapped, they dream and sway.

Beneath the weight of ancient stone,
Untold stories lie alone.
The echoes of their mighty roar,
Once shook the earth; now, lore of yore.

Adorned with jewels, their dreams take flight,
In darkness vast, they guard the night.
Each glimmer holds a saga spun,
Of battles fought and victories won.

In these depths, where shadows spin,
Life's tapestry begins within.
The heart of giants, veiled from sight,
Holds worlds unseen in endless night.

Yet as the dawn spills golden grace,
There stirs a shift in timeless space.
The sun will rise, their dreams will spark,
In mirrored light, from depths to dark.

Requiem for a Sunken Era

In ocean's embrace, where time stands still,
A sunken era, a whispered thrill.
With every wave, a tale unfolds,
Of dreams once bright, now draped in gold.

The coral reefs, their vibrant hue,
Hold memories lost, known to but few.
Once vibrant souls now hushed in dread,
In watery realms, where silence led.

Beneath the tides, the echoes blend,
Of laughter lost and dreams that wend.
Each bubble carries a sigh postponed,
In currents deep, where hopes are honed.

The sunken ships, their stories weave,
Of journeys long and hearts to grieve.
In shadows cast by water's play,
A requiem for what fades away.

Yet in the depths, a spark remains,
Of lives once lived, of joys and pains.
A whispered promise, a gentle tear,
For every heart that held them dear.

The Hidden Path Among the Flames

In shadows deep where embers glow,
A trail unseen begins to show.
With whispered winds, it calls my name,
A dance of sparks, yet not the same.

The flickering light leads the way,
Through labyrinths where the lost may stay.
Each step reveals a tale untold,
Of bravery, of hearts both bold.

From ashes rise the dreams of yore,
A phoenix song, forevermore.
With every turn, a secret waits,
To guide the lost through fire's gates.

Beware the flame, lest you be burned,
For in its warmth, the truth is churned.
Yet with each dusk, the dawn draws near,
A brighter path will soon appear.

In the blaze where shadows leap,
The hidden truths are ours to keep.
A journey forged in smoke and light,
The path ignites the endless night.

Murmurs of Enchantment in the Lair

Deep within the cavern's breath,
A peaceful stillness masks the death.
Murmurs rise, soft and low,
Whispering secrets from below.

The walls are draped in silver sheen,
Where echoes dance, and none have been.
In shadows thick, enchantments weave,
A tapestry that dares deceive.

Soft glowing orbs, like fireflies,
Illuminate the night's disguise.
Each flicker tells a story sweet,
Of love once lost, a heart's defeat.

Beneath the stones, the magic stirs,
It ebbs and flows like gentle purrs.
A symphony of ancient lore,
Inviting dreams to seek the shore.

In slumber deep, the whispers call,
To those who dare to risk the fall.
For in this lair, the wondrous gleams,
Awaken hope from shattered dreams.

The Subtle Gaze of a Cloaked Giant

In twilight's hush, a figure stands,
A cloaked giant with weathered hands.
His gaze, profound, a chilling chill,
With knowledge vast, and heart of will.

Beneath the hood, his eyes could see,
Through veils of time, to destiny.
A silent watcher of human plight,
He knows the shadows of the night.

With gentle grace, he treads the earth,
Where sorrow dwells and dreams give birth.
Though silence reigns, his whispers loom,
A guiding light in darkest gloom.

Each step he takes leaves marks unseen,
A subtle trace where he has been.
With every sigh, the world he bends,
To match the paths where fate descends.

And if you pause and quiet breathe,
You'll sense the magic he can weave.
For in his gaze, the stars align,
To show you paths, unknown, divine.

Vanished Light in the Grayscale

In realms where colors fade to gray,
A light once danced, now swept away.
Memories linger like distant stars,
In the haunting echoes of our scars.

Lost in shadows, we search for hues,
For threads of hope in muted views.
Yet through the fog, a whisper calls,
To lift us up when darkness falls.

The grayscale world conceals the spark,
Where visions thrived, igniting dark.
But in our hearts, the embers glow,
To guide us forth, where rivers flow.

With gentle hands, we paint anew,
Restoring dreams, both bright and true.
In every stroke, resilience sings,
Of brighter days and hidden wings.

So let us seek the vibrant light,
That casts away our silent night.
For even in this muted space,
The vanished light can find its place.

Gossamer Dreams Above the Mountains

In twilight's hush where whispers glide,
Soft gossamer dreams take to the sky.
They dance like echoes on moonlit tides,
A tapestry woven by night's gentle sigh.

Mountains loom proud, their peaks kissed by stars,
Guardians of secrets, of stories untold.
With each breath of night, they soften the scars,
As dreams thread the air like fine strands of gold.

Soft shadows flutter as dreams intertwine,
While shadows embrace the sweet fragrance of night.
The world holds its breath, all secrets divine,
As whispers of longing dance out of sight.

Above the horizon, where starlight gleams,
A symphony swells in the heart of the deep.
In the cradle of night, we weave our sweet dreams,
While mountains stand guard, as we drift into sleep.

So close your weary eyes, let the visions play,
For gossamer dreams are the night's tender gift.
Above the vast mountains, they gently sway,
In the still of the darkness, our spirits they lift.

Specters of Ember in the Dusk

In the embrace of dusk, the embers spark,
Specters of fire dance from shadows of night.
They flicker and fade, like whispers in dark,
Leaving trails of embers, a fleeting delight.

A haunting refrain sings the stars to their home,
As shadows grow long, and the twilight takes flight.
With heartbeats of magic, through darkness we roam,
In this delicate balance of day and of night.

The sky's painted canvas, a symphony bold,
Reflects in our souls, a flickering flame.
With secrets in silence, and stories retold,
In the glow of the dusk, we call out their name.

Cloaked in the twilight, together we stand,
With specters of ember creating our dream.
Through the whispering winds, take my gentle hand,
And weave the bright darkness with hope's flowing beam.

As the night deepens, and shadows descend,
The embers will shimmer, a sweet lonesome song.
In this fleeting moment, where dreams never end,
We embrace the unknowns, where we all belong.

The Mirage of Celestial Claws

In the hush of the night, a mirage appears,
Celestial claws stretch across the wide sky.
They beckon the dreamers, awaken their fears,
In a dance of the cosmos, where thoughts softly fly.

With tints of the stars, and whispers of past,
The shadows of night swathe the world in their grace.
Through the mirror of time, the echoes hold fast,
While wishes take flight, with the moon's soft embrace.

In caverns of silence, where secrets abide,
The mirage of dreams hovers close to the heart.
Each flutter, an omen, with galaxies wide,
As we search for the threads of our souls to impart.

Beneath the soft shimmer, where ancients reside,
The celestial claws draw the cosmos near.
In this quiet moment, our hearts open wide,
To the wonder of night, and all we hold dear.

With each lucid glance, our spirits set free,
The mirage holds stories of worlds yet unknown.
In the web of the night, just you and just me,
We dance with the stars and make the sky our own.

Twilight's Breath on Scaled Horizons

The twilight extends her fingers so neat,
Across scaled horizons, where whispers entwine.
As dragons take wing, their hearts skip a beat,
In the lull of the dusk, where dreams brightly shine.

With scales like the night, reflecting the stars,
They soar through the heavens, wild spirits set free.
Each heartbeat a tale, as they chase their memoirs,
On the breath of the twilight, eternally.

A waltz of the waves, through the sky they will glide,
With twilight as canvas, rich shades intertwine.
These guardians of secrets, no longer can hide,
As the night opens wide, with a heart so divine.

In the hush of the evening, a chorus takes flight,
As the twilight unveils her enchanting domain.
With courage ignited, and hope burning bright,
We leap to the winds, unchained from our pain.

So come to the edge, let your spirit find peace,
In silhouettes soaring on twilight's soft breath.
For the journey is bold, and our hearts will release,
As we stand on the cusp of life, love, and death.

On the Brink of Enchantment's Veil

In twilight's glow, the whispers call,
A dance of shadows, a world enthralled.
Through trees that shimmer, secrets sigh,
Where dreams and echoes learn to fly.

A mist ensnares the wandering heart,
With every step, the magic starts.
In glades adorned with silver light,
The night unfolds, a pure delight.

The moon ascends, a watchful eye,
As fortunes twist and fates rely.
In corners soft, the nightingale sings,
Tales of wonder and hidden things.

A tapestry woven of ancient lore,
Each thread a promise, a chance to explore.
The veil invites with a gentle plea,
To lose ourselves, to simply be.

So linger, dear friend, in this embrace,
For magic lies in every trace.
Let time dissolve in softest shade,
On the brink where dreams are made.

Chronicles Lost in the Veil of Time

Once upon a spark of dawn,
Where echoes of wisdom linger on.
The pages flutter in bittersweet,
Stories entwined in rhythmic beat.

With ink of stars and whispers hushed,
The chronicles sing, a life that's flushed.
In shadows deep, where legends play,
The past and future dance, sway away.

Each chapter opens a door anew,
A tapestry woven with different hue.
In realms unseen, the echoes roam,
Mapping the heart to its destined home.

Time's gentle hand, it sweeps aside,
Memories lost in the soft tide.
Yet every moment, cherished and bright,
Birthing the tales spun in the night.

So grasp these tales of ages passed,
For in their weave, our fates are cast.
In the veil of time, let hopes unfurl,
As our stories merge in this wondrous swirl.

The Silent Roar of Foggy Realms

In fog's embrace, the world stands still,
A whispered roar beneath the hill.
Each breath of mist, a secret sworn,
As dreams awaken, fragile, torn.

The trees are cloaked with silent might,
Guardians of shadows, keeping the night.
With every pulse, the earth does sigh,
In foggy realms where spirits lie.

A phantom echo, a flicker here,
Where time bends gently, drawing near.
The heartbeats echo, soft and slow,
In this realm where wild wonders flow.

The labyrinths weave through thoughts and fears,
In silent roars, the wisdom nears.
Each step reveals what once was lost,
In fog's embrace, we count the cost.

So wanderer, heed the call of mist,
In every flurry, there's magic kissed.
For in the silence, treasures awake,
The roar of fog, our souls to shake.

When Light Meets Legendary Beasts

When dawn breaks wide, the wild awakes,
With legends old, the world it makes.
In every glade, a flicker bright,
Where dreams entwine with ancient night.

The beasts of lore in colors bold,
In shimmering light, their tales unfold.
From feathered wings to scales that gleam,
In each heartbeat, a shared dream.

With whispers soft, they grace the air,
Keeping watch on dreams laid bare.
In every rustle, a promise held,
Of journeys where the brave have dwelled.

The sunbeams dance on emerald leaves,
Where magic breathes and heart believes.
In light's embrace, the legends shine,
Where hearts and worlds and dreams align.

So wander forth to realms untamed,
When light meets beasts, the wild reclaimed.
For in this union, dreams take flight,
With legendary friends, the future bright.

Faint Echoes Beneath the Scales

In twilight's grip, whispers creep,
Beneath the scales where secrets sleep.
A flicker here, a shadow there,
Faint echoes dance through evening air.

In depths of waters cold and clear,
Mysteries call, the brave draw near.
They seek the truth, with hearts of fire,
Yet find themselves in deep mire.

With every splash, a tale unfolds,
Of ancient dreams and legends old.
The drumming heart, the silent plea,
Calls forth the brave to search the sea.

Each scale that shimmers hides a spark,
A piece of light within the dark.
The creatures watch with knowing eyes,
As stardust mingles with the skies.

Yet caution reigns in waters deep,
For fates entwined in shadows creep.
In search of wisdom, tread with care,
For whispers weave the tales they bear.

Enigmatic Spirits of the Skyline

Upon the heights where eagles soar,
Spirits linger, forevermore.
When day gives way to night's embrace,
They dance in veils of moonlit grace.

In twilight's hue, their laughter rings,
A symphony of whispered things.
Each fleeting glance, a story spun,
In colors bright as setting sun.

Beneath the stars, their forms take flight,
Enigmas veiled in silken night.
Through wisps of clouds, they weave and dart,
With secrets held within their heart.

A gentle breeze, a rustling leaf,
In every sigh, a hidden grief.
For time has taught them, love and loss,
As burdened souls, they count the cost.

Yet in their dance, there's joy profound,
In every twirl, a hope unbound.
For every spirit gracing the skies,
Dreams linger long, and never die.

Lurking Shadows Beneath the Clouds

In folds of grey where shadows dwell,
A whispered tale of secret spell.
With every gust, a laugh, a moan,
Lurking figures, forever alone.

Through misty paths, they wander wide,
Their silent laughs in darkness hide.
For every heart that beats with dread,
They're merely thoughts that dance in head.

Yet in their depths, a truth does lie,
To face your fears, let courage fly.
With heavy hearts, the lost return,
In shadows' grasp, there's much to learn.

Each swirling cloud, a tale to share,
Of dreams that falter, souls laid bare.
But through the night, the dawn must rise,
As light breaks forth to part the skies.

A journey made, both dark and bright,
Within the shadows, fears take flight.
So fear not what the night may hold,
The shadows whisper tales untold.

Ethereal Glow on Charred Wings

When dusk descends with smoldering grace,
A glow ignites in a sorrowed place.
From ashes rise the dreams once lost,
With wings of fire, they dare the cost.

In every ember's flicker bright,
A memory dances in the night.
Charred wings spread wide, they soar anew,
With hope that shines in vibrant hue.

They learn to chase the fading light,
To weave through shadows, find their flight.
Each scorched feather, a testament,
Of battles fought and lives well spent.

Through tempest winds, they find their song,
An anthem of where the brave belong.
Each note a pledge to rise again,
From smoldering past, they break the chain.

Ethereal glow, a guiding fire,
Awakens dreams that never tire.
With every flap of charred delight,
They summon forth the coming light.

Veils of Mist in the Twilight Realm

In twilight's breath, soft whispers call,
Veils of mist begin to fall.
Secrets dance in fading light,
Enchantments weave through coming night.

Shadows stretch with grace and care,
Mysterious tales float in the air.
Each heart beats to a hidden tune,
Under the watch of a rising moon.

Beyond the woods, the owls do hoot,
While crickets serenade with a delicate lute.
Night unfurls her velvet cloak,
Embracing all that words have spoke.

Stars flicker in a velvet sea,
Mirroring dreams that dare to be.
In this realm, where spirits roam,
Every shadow feels like home.

So linger here, in this hushed place,
Let the night reveal her face.
For in the mists of twilight's grace,
We find our hearts' true resting space.

Shimmering Shadows on Scales of Time

Upon the river's shimmering flow,
Shadows flicker, come and go.
Each ripple holds a tale untold,
A tapestry of dreams to behold.

Scales of time glisten bright,
In fading echoes, day meets night.
Moments dance like fireflies,
In the embrace of starry skies.

Memories linger in twilight's edge,
Whispers wrapped in every pledge.
The past and future intertwine,
In the depths where dreams align.

Glimmers of laughter, glimpses of tears,
Carried through the weave of years.
In this realm where shadows play,
Time stands still, then fades away.

So ponder here, on the shimmering tide,
As time's soft luminescence guides.
For in the shadows, we shall find,
The echoes of our heart and mind.

Echoes Beneath the Glistening Peaks

In heights where whispers live and breathe,
Echoes forge the paths we weave.
Beneath the peaks with crowns of snow,
Stories of ages start to flow.

Each rock, each stone, a silent friend,
Guarding secrets that never end.
The mountain's pulse, steady and strong,
Holds the echo of every song.

Skies of amber fade to gray,
As shadows dance at close of day.
In this embrace, we find our grace,
Lost in the timeless, sacred space.

Whispers hang in the mountain air,
Carried on winds that do not care.
The glistening peaks, they call our names,
A realm untouched by earthly claims.

So stand with me, on this lofty ground,
Where echoes of the past abound.
In the silence, we shall see,
The beauty of eternity.

Wisps of Enchantment in the Dusk

As dusk descends with tender hues,
Wisps of magic gently fuse.
The air, alive with whispered dreams,
Embraces all with silent screams.

Fireflies twinkle, soft and bright,
Guiding wanderers into night.
In this realm where shadows play,
We'll lose ourselves and drift away.

Each breath a promise, a fleeting chance,
In twilight's glow, we dare to dance.
Time slips softly, like fine sand,
While secrets float on a silver strand.

Enchantments linger, thick and sweet,
In twilight's grasp, our souls compete.
For in this wisp of enchanting dusk,
Lies the magic that we trust.

So follow me through layers thick,
Into the night where dreams can stick.
Together, we shall find our fates,
In the dusk where magic waits.

The Subtle Dance of Twilight's Fire

In the glow of day's last kiss,
Where shadows weave with twilight's grace,
Whispers of embers swirl and twist,
As stars ignite in their embrace.

A flicker beneath the ancient trees,
Caught in the sigh of the evening breeze,
The world turns soft, the light draws near,
In the hush of dusk, we shed our fear.

Cascading gold from the sun's embrace,
Dancing sparks in a glowing space,
Twilight's fire flickers, ever bright,
Guiding lost souls through the night.

With every pulse, the darkness swells,
Into the night where the magic dwells,
Holding secrets in the velvet air,
A promise wrapped in twilight's care.

So let us waltz in this fleeting hour,
Beneath the stars, we'll claim our power,
For in the dusk, true hearts will find,
The subtle dance of the intertwined.

Fertile Shadows of the Serpent's Realm

Beneath the boughs where secrets coil,
In shadows deep the ancients toil,
Where whispered myths and legends blend,
The serpent's realm shall never end.

Rich are the lands where the twilight spills,
Nurtured by dreams and enchanted thrills,
The fertile ground, lush and alive,
Holds tales of magic, waiting to thrive.

A flick of the tongue, a knowing glance,
In the depths of gloom, the shadows dance,
Echoes of wisdom from ages past,
In the serpent's embrace, we are steadfast.

Branches entwined like faithful friends,
Guarding the mysteries that nature lends,
With every rustle, stories take flight,
In shadows, the heartbeat of the night.

So wander deep through fertile dreams,
Where nothing is ever as it seems,
For in these shadows, truth reveals,
The serpent's charm, the world it heals.

Gliding Through a Veil of Chill

Under the arc of a frosty moon,
Whispers echo a haunting tune,
A mist that cloaks the sleeping ground,
In this stillness, magic is found.

Moonlit figures glide with grace,
Through the veil where shadows trace,
Breath of winter, crisp and clear,
Cradling secrets, drawing near.

Where frost flowers bloom upon the trees,
Entwined in dreams upon the breeze,
A dance of spirits in the fray,
Gliding through night to greet the day.

With every step, the chill reveals,
The hidden wonders that winter seals,
An icy tapestry, vast and grand,
A lullaby sung by nature's hand.

So wander forth into the night,
Where magic shimmers, pure and bright,
In this veil of chill, hearts take flight,
Gliding softly into the light.

The Fading Light on Dragon's Breath

At twilight's edge where shadows creep,
Upon the mount where secrets sleep,
The dragon's breath, a fiery glow,
Wanes softly as the night winds blow.

Crimson hues in the fading sky,
Wrap twilight's heart with a gentle sigh,
Beneath the watch of ancient stone,
The tales of glory and sorrow have grown.

With every ember that starts to fade,
Whispers of battles, the price was paid,
Yet beauty lingers in the night's embrace,
In dragon's breath, we find our place.

As stars emerge to claim their throne,
The echoes linger, a somber tone,
In the fading light, stories unwind,
Unraveling threads of the intertwined.

So heed the whispers of the night,
In the shadows, find your light,
For though the glow may dim and cease,
In the fading dusk, we find our peace.

The Twilight Veil of the Ancient Kin

In the twilight glow where shadows creep,
Whispers of old awaken from sleep.
Ancient kin in the fragile light,
Guardians of secrets, cloaked in night.

Beneath the stars, their stories flow,
Tales of enchantment in ages aglow.
The moon, she weaves her silver thread,
Binding the past to the paths we tread.

Leaves flutter softly as breezes sigh,
Echoes of laughter, the night's lullaby.
In the hush of dusk, their laughter rings,
A song of magic that time softly brings.

Old stones remember the dreams once dreamed,
In twilight's embrace, nothing is as it seemed.
With every heartbeat, the veil draws thin,
The twilight whispers of the ancient kin.

Through the veil of dusk, their spirits dance,
Inviting us gently, a wondrous chance.
To glimpse the magic that lies beyond,
In twilight's embrace, we weave our bond.

Embrace of the Dimmed Void

In the embrace of shadows deep,
Where the lost together weep.
A haunting chill wraps around tight,
Swallowed by the absence of light.

In echoes soft, the silence speaks,
Of forgotten hopes and dreamt-of peaks.
Veils of darkness, like creeping vines,
Entwine the hearts where sorrow shines.

In the depths of the dimmed void place,
We search for light, yet lose our grace.
Treading softly on whispered fears,
Dancing between the mist and tears.

Yet through the darkness, a glimmer calls,
A flicker of hope within the walls.
For even shadows must someday fade,
And light may find the path we've made.

So let us hold, with trembling hands,
The fragile dreams that darkness spands.
Embrace the void, for in it lies,
The strength to rise beneath the skies.

Shimmering Haze on the Mystic Edge

On the mystic edge where dreams unfold,
A shimmering haze, a tale retold.
Stars drip like honey from skies so high,
Painting the canvas of night's soft sigh.

Waves of magic ripple through the air,
Inviting the brave without a care.
In this realm where time twists and bends,
Every moment sparks, and eternity blends.

Whispers of wonder dance on the breeze,
Calling us forth with ethereal ease.
The pulse of the earth in tandem sings,
A melody woven of ancient things.

Flickering lights in the twilight glow,
Guide wandering souls with a gentle flow.
In this enchanted, shimmering haze,
Every path leads to infinite ways.

So tread softly on this sacred ground,
Let your spirit soar, let your heart be found.
In the shimmering haze on the mystic edge,
Find the truth beyond the treacherous ledge.

Flickering Echoes Across the Misty Expanse

Across the expanse where mists unfurl,
Flickering echoes of a forgotten world.
Silent footfalls upon the ancient path,
Whispers of legends invoke the past.

In the twilight glow, shadows entwine,
Each flicker of light, a forgotten sign.
The air thrums soft with promises lost,
As memories beckon, no matter the cost.

The mist blankets the land, thick and warm,
Protecting the secrets from every storm.
An ethereal dance of light and fog,
A flicker of truth in a swirling bog.

Within the haze, stories await,
To guide the lost toward their fate.
Hands reaching out, hearts open wide,
In flickering echoes, our souls coincide.

So follow the whispers, let them in,
Let flickering echoes be your kin.
For across the misty expanse lies,
A world reborn beneath the skies.

Glimmers of Fire Through the Fog

In early morn, where shadows creep,
The firelight dances, secrets to keep.
Through veils of mist, its glow does weave,
A tale of hope for those who believe.

Whispers of warmth in the chilling air,
A flicker of courage, dissipating despair.
The embers spark bright in the twilight haze,
Guiding the lost through the fog's embrace.

Each flicker a promise, a journey to find,
The heart's own beacon, forever entwined.
As shadows retreat from the dawn's soft light,
The fire shall guide with its bold, gentle might.

Yet danger lurks in the harboring grey,
Foes in the shadows that seek to betray.
But the glimmers of fire will pierce through the night,
With strong, steadfast hearts that will stand up and fight.

So heed the flame and let it ignite,
The dreams in your heart; let them take flight.
For even in fog, where darkness may reign,
There's magic to find — an eternal flame.

Secrets Untold in the Murky Air

In the depths of the night, the secrets lie,
Woven in whispers, beneath the dark sky.
Murky air thickens with tales of the past,
Each word a spell that holds shadows fast.

Beneath the stillness, a promise awaits,
Hidden in echoes of forgotten fates.
A tingle of magic, an unsolved riddle,
Stirs the forgotten, the lost in the middle.

Breathe deep the essence that tinges the night,
For magic is cloaked, but it yearns for the light.
With courage, draw near, let your heart lead the way,
To the stories untold, where the brave dare to stay.

Through misty embraces, the truth swirls around,
In fragments of laughter and sorrow profound.
Listen closely, for the world whispers true,
In the murky air, a new path to pursue.

And under the stars, what wonders unfold,
When souls yearn for secrets, so daring and bold.
In the silence, a promise, a bond will be cast,
Within the heart's echo, the future holds fast.

The Drifting Mists of Forgotten Legends

Beneath the waves of the moonlit glow,
Drift echoes of heroes, long lost in the flow.
Mists cradle tales, so ancient, so dear,
Whispering softly for all who will hear.

In the depths of the night, where shadows do play,
The legends awaken, refusing to stay.
Each story a journey, a map made of dreams,
Guided by starlight that shimmer and beams.

Warriors brave, with spirits untouched,
Carved their names deep, in legends clutched.
Through tempest and trial, their echoes remain,
While the mists sweep softly, like whispers of rain.

So gather the scraps of the tales rich and bright,
For in every heartbeat, a flicker of light.
The drifting mists hold eternity's grace,
In the dance of remembrance, find your own place.

Embrace the unknown, let your spirit take flight,
For wisdom lies wrapped in the folds of the night.
In the heart of the legends, find courage anew,
And follow the mists, where your own dreams come true.

Obscured Majesties of the Firebrand

In the glow of the flames where shadows lie cast,
Majesties dance, obscured by the past.
The firebrand flickers, a force bold and bright,
Shaping the stories that flicker in light.

Draw near to the warmth, let your heart feel the heat,
For in the embers, the past and present meet.
With courage ignited, let spirits arise,
In the realm of the flames, where magic never dies.

The centuries whisper of battles and peace,
A tapestry woven that never shall cease.
Each spark holds a memory, forgotten yet grand,
In the heart of the fire, lies the tales of the land.

Through smoke and through flame, the visions appear,
Obscured in the ashes, yet ever so near.
The firebrand beckons with secrets unspun,
Inviting all seekers to know what's begun.

So trust in the glow, let the journeys unfold,
For within the great circle lies wisdom untold.
The obscured majesties await in the fire,
An endless connection that never will tire.

Breath of the Elders in Twilight's Cusp

In shadows thick, the ancients stir,
Whispers flow like a gentle blur.
With twilight's grace, they weave their song,
To keep the lost where they belong.

Through mossy paths and silvery beams,
They guard the tales of forgotten dreams.
A flicker of light, a shimmer of hope,
As elder roots entwine and grope.

Beneath the arch of a twilight sky,
The spirits dance, their voices fly.
A warmth that holds the past's embrace,
In every breath, the timeless grace.

The evening deepens, the stars awake,
A tapestry in silver and jade.
In the heart of night, their secrets blend,
As age-old wisdom refuses to end.

Gathered dreams beneath a spell,
In silence shared, where shadows dwell.
For in the cusp of night and day,
The elders breathe, and stars obey.

The Sublime Dusk of Echoing Roars

When dusk descends on forest's throne,
The wild hearts stir, their voices known.
With echoing roars that split the air,
A primal song, both fierce and rare.

The canopy sways to the rhythm's beat,
As shadows meld with twilight's heat.
Beneath the boughs, where legends breathe,
The echoes hold what earth conceives.

A symphony sung by the twilight breeze,
Where ancient spirits find their ease.
They linger long in the dusk's embrace,
In every roar, a trace of grace.

With every note, a story told,
Of brave young hearts and heroes bold.
They dance with flames that flicker bright,
In the sublime dusk, they take to flight.

As stars ignite the velvet sky,
The echoes swirl, they soar and sigh.
In phantom echoes, the night aligns,
And in their song, all magic shines.

Luminous Enigma of the Ember Clan

Upon the hearth, where embers glow,
The clan of fire makes secrets flow.
In radiant light, their laughter rings,
A luminous tale that twilight brings.

With grace they move in a dance divine,
In shadows cast, their fates entwine.
Each flicker tells of battles past,
Of brave souls forged to forever last.

The flickering flame, a guiding guide,
In every flicker, a world resides.
Within their hearts, the ember's glow,
The fire's song, a constant flow.

As night unfolds, their spirits soar,
In the luminous warmth, they seek for more.
With whispered tales and laughter shared,
The Ember Clan, beyond compare.

Through glowing coals, their legends dart,
Filling the night with fearless heart.
And in the depths of ember's grace,
They find the light of their embrace.

Mists That Veil the Golden Scales

In mists that shuffle upon the ground,
Golden scales in silence abound.
With every breath, the secrets bloom,
Where ancient dreams find room to loom.

Draped in shadows of twilight's weave,
The guardians watch, their hearts believe.
They shimmer bright in the veils of night,
Each glistening scale a beacon of light.

Through softest fog, their stories flow,
A tapestry spun by time's soft glow.
In whispered breaths, the past ignites,
The mists reveal what hides from sights.

As soft winds carry the echoes near,
The golden scales beckon those who hear.
In twilight's hush, the hearts awake,
In realms of mist, no bond can break.

With every shimmer, the worlds align,
In mists that weave, their fates entwine.
For in the fog, the past commands,
The golden scales in ancient hands.

Murky Horizons of the Wandering Soul

In shadows deep where phantoms dwell,
A wandering soul weaves silent spells.
With every step on paths untread,
Hope flickers dim, though not yet dead.

Through misty fields and haunting wails,
The heart beats on, though fear prevails.
Each whispered name, a beckoning call,
A ghostly dance within the thrall.

Yet in the dark, a spark does glow,
A light to guide where shadows flow.
With every twist of fate's cruel thread,
A tale unfolds of the brave and dead.

The horizon calls, a tempest's roar,
Through murk and gloom to a distant shore.
The soul must wander, never rest,
For in the unknown lies its quest.

As dawn breaks free from night's embrace,
The wandering soul finds its place.
In murky depths, the truth unfolds,
A tale of dreams and love retold.

Serenity Swallowed by the Nightshade

Beneath the moon, in silent bloom,
The nightshade casts away the gloom.
Whispers soft, like velvet skies,
Serenity falls as daylight dies.

In shadowed corners, secrets creep,
Where worries fade and lost souls weep.
A tranquil heart begins to dance,
In night's embrace, a haunted trance.

Yet in that calm, a warning breathes,
For darkness feeds on tangled wreaths.
With every sigh, a moment lost,
True peace can vanish at a cost.

Yet look within the velvet shroud,
For strength lies still amidst the crowd.
Serenity, though fleeting, stays,
A flicker of light in shadowed ways.

As nightshade's grip begins to wane,
Heartbeats echo through the pain.
For every dusk that shadows grace,
A dawn awaits, a fresh embrace.

Flames That Flicker in Twilight's Grasp

In twilight's glow, where shadows play,
Flickers of hope dance and sway.
A fire ignites in whispered hues,
Chasing the darkness, the heart renews.

From ember's warmth, a tale unfolds,
Of dreams forgotten and legends told.
In every flicker, a secret hides,
A brightness bound where mystery bides.

Yet time is fleeting, soft, and rare,
Each flame a wish upon the air.
To chase the dark, to hold the light,
A fragile heart within the night.

The stars above, they twinkle low,
Crafting a tapestry of woe.
But within that weave, the flames will rise,
Their brilliance seen through endless skies.

As twilight wraps its gentle shroud,
The flames stand tall, defiant, proud.
In every heart, a spark shall last,
A testament to shadows cast.

The Ethereal Embrace of the Dying Day

The sun bows low, a golden sphere,
In hues of crimson, amber, clear.
An ethereal light in twilight's grasp,
A fleeting moment, too precious to clasp.

As day meets night in gentle sighs,
The world awakens, while silence lies.
In fading warmth, the shadows play,
An embrace soft as words we say.

The whispers of dusk, they beckon near,
With every breath, a promise clear.
In the dying glow, all fears unwind,
A tender peace for a troubled mind.

Yet time drifts on, a thief so sly,
As stars arise to claim the sky.
Embrace the dusk, let worries part,
For in each ending, a new day starts.

With every heartbeat, the day recedes,
An ethereal dance, where longing leads.
In the twilight's arms, we softly sway,
In the tender embrace of the dying day.

www.ingramcontent.com/pod-product-compliance
Ingram Content Group UK Ltd.
Pitfield, Milton Keynes, MK11 3LW, UK
UKHW021501280125
4335UKWH00035B/643

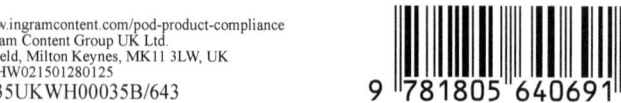